This symbol—three plumes of

steam rising from a pool of hot

water—indicates hot springs

on Japanese maps and is often

displayed at the entrance of public

baths and hot springs.

The Japanese phonetic

character yu means "hot water"

and is often displayed at the

entrance of public baths.

How To Take A
Japanese Bath

by Leonard Koren
illustrations by Suehiro Maruo

Stone Bridge Press
Berkeley, California

Contents

Introduction

If there are but few things that can be
called uniquely Japanese living culture,
Japanese-style bathing is certainly one
of them.

In Japan, clean and dirty are absolute and
irreconcilable notions. Thus the Japanese
logic of cleanliness dictates two parts to
the bathing ritual: first washing and then
soaking. Body washing involves soaping,
scrubbing, and rinsing body dirt away.
Soaking consists of doing nothing except
sitting quietly and enjoying the moment.

The procedures outlined in this book
apply to Japanese-style bathing anywhere
in Japan: at home, at public baths, and at
hot spring resorts.

1

Any time is a fine time to enjoy
a Japanese bath: on rising in the
morning, before retiring at night,
or whenever the inspiration
enters your mind.

2

Whether for bathing at home or at
a public bathhouse, your bath kit
should include: soap, shampoo, a
washcloth, clean underwear and
socks . . . and a plastic bucket
for scooping water. The bucket
doubles as a handy container
for the other kit items, and is
especially useful when strolling
to the public bath.

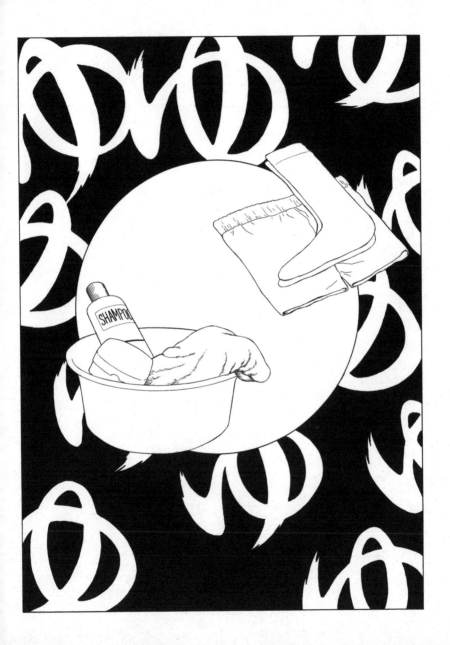

3

To prepare the bath, first fill the tub with hot water, testing it with your hand to make sure it's the right temperature for you. When the tub is full, stir the water with your hand or a stirring paddle to blend the hot water on top with the cooler water that tends to sink to the bottom.

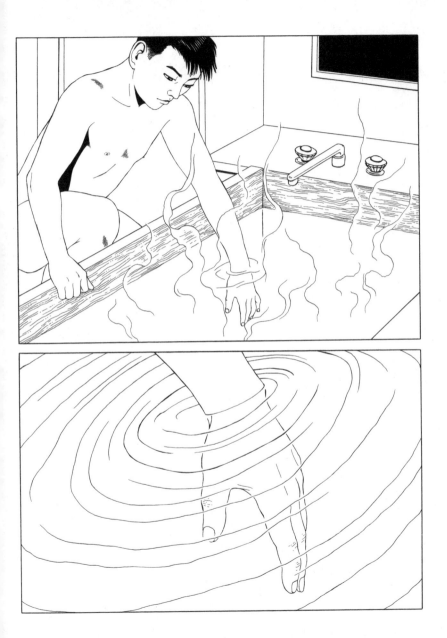

4

With the plastic bucket, scoop
some water from the tub and pour
it over your torso to rinse off
surface dirt. Continue scooping
and pouring, being sure to rinse
your private parts and anywhere
that it is especially grimy, like
your feet. Many people wash with
soap at this stage, but the choice
is yours. Just remember that the
cleaner you are, the cleaner the
water will be for the next
person who enters the bath.
Do be considerate.

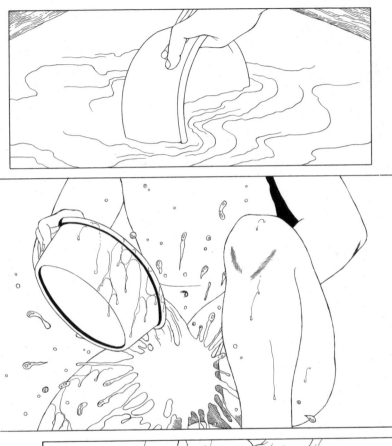

5

Gingerly, ease into the steaming
bath and sit quietly.

6

Soak until your body is
heated thoroughly, and then
get out carefully.

7

Using water from a wall faucet or scooped from the tub, lather up your washcloth with soap and scrub yourself until you're squeaky clean. This is also the time to shampoo your hair if you wish. Whatever you do, be careful not to get any soap or suds into the bath water.

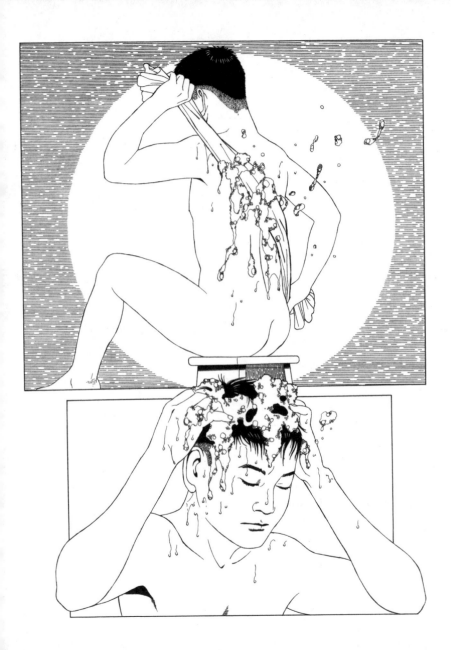

8

With fresh water from the tub or
wall faucet, thoroughly rinse
all the soap and shampoo
from your body.

9

Ease back into the tub and enjoy
a good long soak. Feel your body
relax and any stress dissipate.
Pure bliss!

10

Bathing Japanese-style is often a
communal activity where gentle
conversation is an added pleasure.
Sometimes you share a bath with
your family. And sometimes,
at a public bath or hot springs
resort, you bathe with complete
strangers. Public baths are usually
divided into separate pools for
men and women, but if you find
yourself in a unisex bath, all
you have to do is cover yourself
modestly with your washcloth
when walking around and
otherwise bathe as usual.

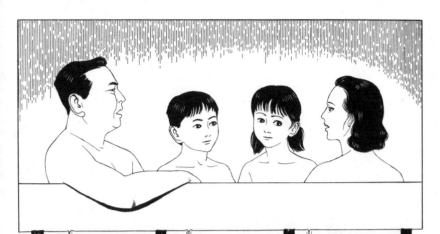

松の湯

11

As a courtesy to the next bather,
skim any hair or debris off the
surface of the water with a net
when you are done. Then place the
insulated cover on the tub to help
keep the water hot. The next
bather may add piping hot water
to replace any that was scooped
out or to increase the water
temperature. Some Japanese
bathtubs have built-in heaters that
allow the water to be reheated
while you soak or before the
following day's bath. Many
ecologically minded households
recycle the bathwater after
everyone in the family has bathed,
using it for the first cycle in the
washing machine, for watering the
garden, and so on.

12

Après bath is a time for relaxing
and cooling off. So find a
comfortable spot where you can
sit calmly and let magnificent
thoughts fill your mind.

Bathing in Japan has always been
more about getting pure than about
getting clean. After all, the act of
scrubbing the body free of dirt
always takes place outside the tub.
Only after the body is clean does
the bather finally enter the water.

In ancient times—1,000 years ago—
the "bath" was a natural hot pool, one of
thousands created by Japan's proximity to
a tectonic crash zone. Then the impurities
exorcised by the bath were such things
as death, disease, and menstrual blood.
Today, the typical Japanese tub is a
hollow of molded plastic and fiberglass,
located indoors, and just big enough to
sit in with your legs folded up to your
chin. Still, the object is the same—not
simply to rid yourself of the befoulment
of the physical world but to cleanse the
mind and spirit until the body is in tune

with the forces of Nature. In the West, one works to avoid sin and to attain God's glory in the next life. In Japan, spiritual dirt is something that attaches to us all—like the reek of hair pomade or tobacco smoke—in the course of living, and can be easily removed by a daily bath.

Records show that Buddhist temples in the 8th century maintained steam baths, sponsored in part by donations from wealthy nobles hoping to gain spiritual merit. The wealthy would personally assist in the bathing of the poor and sick, urged on by the example of the beautiful Empress Komyo. The empress was said to have a light emanating from her, indicating her high spiritual advancement. One day the light went out. She attributed this to her own lack of devotion and swore to bathe one thousand of the impoverished and infirm of all ages and sexes. The last person who came to her was a leper—or perhaps the Buddha

disguised as a leper. But the empress
did not hesitate, and upon bathing
him immediately her aura returned.

The first commercial public bath—
or *sento*—was built in the 1590s, and
entrepreneurs throughout the country
soon were opening up their own
bathhouses. Food, conversation, games,
and sexual pleasures became a part of
the bath scene. Water replaced steam.
In the late 19th century the government
banned mixed-sex bathing. But the
sento remained the equivalent of the
medieval European well—the place where
the community gathered to see and be
seen, to exchange news and gossip.

With the construction of modern
housing, the *sento* is disappearing at a
rapid rate from urban Japan. But many
thousand still exist. Many have attached
laundromats, so that your clothes can
soak at the same time you do. Public
baths are generally open from four in
the afternoon until midnight. In their

egalitarian atmosphere you can get warm, chat with your neighbors (many of whom have baths at home but come to enjoy the *sento* anyway), and enjoy a generous volume of architectural space. Often there is a striking mural of a street scene or landscape on the back wall that you can lose yourself in as you sink into the tub.

Almost every *sento* adheres to the same basic plan: At the entrance you remove your shoes. Then you walk beyond a curtain or sliding door to the men's or women's side, where you pay the attendant the equivalent of three or four dollars. Then you undress and, with your bath kit (shampoo, washcloth, etc.), move on to the washing and soaking area.

A more naturalistic version of the *sento* can be found at any of the three thousand or so hot springs (*onsen*) throughout the Japanese countryside. The bathing environment here usually includes a sensitive use of wood, stone, and other natural elements such as ferns and waterfalls. *Onsen* baths usually have men's and women's sections, but the farther you go from the big cities, the less important are divisions by gender. When the baths are actually outdoors (*rotenburo*) there is often no separation between the sexes at all. Here, a deft use of the *tenugui,* an elongated cotton washcloth, provides as much modesty as is required. (After the bath, this same washcloth is used as a drying towel—wrung out and used over and over again like a sponge on the body.)

The home bath is an altogether different experience, since it is solitary and confined. Perhaps it is a metaphor for the nuclearization of the Japanese family, and as such its ascendancy may have dire consequences for the traditional culture. Drawing a full bath every day when a shower would do, particularly if you're living alone, is what the Japanese call *mendokusai*: a bother. But the old ways die hard, and this is immediately noticeable even in the most modern Japanese apartment: the vulgar toilet is almost always in a different compartment from where the body is bathed and purified. The bath in Japan remains that special place where the mind is cleansed as the body steeps in its own physicality.

NOTE: The Japanese word for bath is *furo*. Water is kept very hot in most Japanese baths, much hotter than in the conventional American hot tub. If you are pregnant, older, or have any serious medical—particularly heart- or circulation-related—problems, check with a physician about the advisability of Japanese-style bathing. ALSO: Although Japanese revelers sometimes consume alcoholic beverages prior to bathing, particularly at *onsen* inns, this is not recommended.

The Japanese phonetic character yu *means "hot water" and is often displayed at the entrance of public baths.*

This symbol—three plumes of

steam rising from a pool of hot

water—indicates hot springs

on Japanese maps and is often

displayed at the entrance of public

baths and hot springs.